The Dedalus Press

In Out Of The Rain

Dolores Stewart

IN
OUT OF THE RAIN

Dolores Stewart

1999

DEDALUS

The Dedalus Press
24 The Heath
Cypress Downs
Dublin 6W
Ireland

4.2.00

ISBN 1 901233 42 1 (paper)
ISBN 1 901233 43 X (bound)

Dedalus Press books are represented and distributed in the
U.S.A. and Canada by **Dufour Editions Ltd.**, P.O. Box 7,
Chester Springs, Pennsylvania 19425
and in the UK by **Central Books**, 99 Wallis Road, London
E9 5LN

The Dedalus Press receives financial assistance from
An Chomhairle Ealaíon, The Arts Council, Ireland.

Printed in Dublin by Colour Books Ltd

CONTENTS

Shadows

Cafarnach. Meaning drizzle. As if something caught
in the throat jarred in the small holding
of your song; all the acres of longing
carried on the ebbtide by a blessed candle
on a plaited mat going out in search of the drowned
trapped by submerged rocks or seawrack.

Scattered on the foreshore, the old and broken
rock themselves back from the edge to rise up
out of the old workings of spent tides and *sean-nós*
and the hint of a whisper coming through.
In the face of night, your solace comes from turf fires
and from autumn wildfires on distant mountains,
from the mist clearing, and the open slopes
where clay infers the last toss of light. As dew drops. *Solas.*

• *Cafarnach* = drizzle • *Solas* = light • *Sean-nós* = traditional singing.

Inis Meáin

For all the hours God sent, I could have sat where I did
on the upper deck looking back into the slipstream
and coining new colours for the fabric of the furrows
unearthed by hidden propellors, and the tang
and the salt tears for what was passing.
I see you again, in slow motion, handing me
that single spray of honeysuckle, giving life
to words that reach me across the old language
worn as white cambric in your throat
taking nothing for granted in its fragrance
or in the way you turn to the offshore island
to look for rain or mist coming down the slopes,
a catch in your voice and vowels stunning
as hammer blows to a lost psyche;
an old sense gone missing and almost given up on.

It's not day, love. It's not yet day,
                              nor any danger of it.
It's not day, my dearest love.
                       Look, the night gives no sign.

• "It's not Day" : *Níl sé ina Lá* traditional song

Galileo

Did you feel the earth move, Galileo
kneeling to the cold stone of their idolatry;
the dulled and savage mind

that called you twice a liar, a sacrifice
to crossed stars; their eyes glittering
in that other dark.

You followed the line of that hand
reaching into space, presuming touch;
misjudged the mathematics of their minds.

Hypotheses of glass
shattered galaxies of darkness, fired
imagination in a new crucible.

It was no small matter —
taking the earth from beneath them, stars
above their heads, walls from their world.

Exposure made them terrible and mad,
forced you to your knees, Galileo —

Consider again the stooped sky,
the dumping ground,
stamp your hobbled foot upon the earth.

Don't you know, beyond a shadow, that it moves, it moves?

Lough Derg Sequence

[Lough Derg : place of pilgrimage in the Christian world since
the Early Middle Ages, ranking alongside Canterbury and Com-
postella. The modern pilgrim goes barefoot and fasts for three
days, keeps vigil over one night and completes penitential
exercises while on the island]

I

It's evening on the lough.
Lightheaded clouds shuffle the waters.
The boat resumes its crossing, moving smoothly
in stillness
and arrives.

I renounce the World, the Flesh and the Devil.

Some make it out to be older than Canterbury,
Compostella or Roncevalles,
bells passing for a glimmer
in the dead of winter, twigs snapping
in the underworld;
Dante's swan song, Patrick's last prayer.

Footloose, and for good measure I feel
the texture of sprung earth and get the wind
of an age-old oratorio,
inferring dis-enchantment
through the prism of ankles —
their fragility and sweat;

a barefoot journey, a station,
a clogged compass spinning like a top.

I seal off the darkroom sanctuary, checking
for stray shadows. By the red glow
of the safe light, I slide a page
of white paper into the tank, and agitate.
The image rises, may it please God, faint
at first but looming on a count of eight,
time to stop the clock to measure definition
in the range of greys; then fix it,
not a split second too soon,
a gradient caught, an image saved.

II

It's my deal. I grip the well-thumbed deck
of cards, shuffle and flick them in a peacock's tailspan.
I box the cards and palm them out for a cut
on account of fair play and with all eyes straining
I deal each hand clockwise smacking one card
on another, face down

as footsteps follow suit on the stone beds
shuffling raw deals out of existence.
I stake the credo — first outside
then on the rim, then inside,
then play it again before I call trumps,
play the ace of hearts
on a fast wagered in the early hours
to see sin off
run like the sweat running off him
running off the Cross.

On the rebound, I listen in
as winds strip the penitentials

of all the grim discarded droppings
of every kind of sin, imagine
Mary astray,
salve regina of the go-between,
tackler of bad breath,
Galahad in the Waste Land,
lady of the lough,

as high above, a single bird —
fixed on a distant aria —
strikes hard across a pewter sky
where silence makes a play
beyond the ordered tournaments of prayer.

I wash my face in the invisible
like the wounded Fisher King waiting
for the question of his life.

III

As the spotlight goes down low
into expectations of some fabulous alchemy,
my feet follow actors
finding their feet in the syllables of a dumbshow.

Visibility dips and sways, sees time back into eternity.
Style rainfalls to the manner of rags
and all the small deformities of the footshod
fumble through the moodmusic of stillness:
murmured polyphonies fit to take the strain
of shadows wheeling
like the joker in the pack.
I watch, adrift in a vigil, the stained glass
drain to metallic black.

Was it something I whispered or said aloud
(now is the time the dead walk)
that brought one on, his back to the gable —
a prince of Breffni, surefooted haunter
of pilgrim places, here while his wife marked
the gambled dreams of a trumped king
forced to renege his hand to Norman knights
whose master craftsmen would soon forge
newfangled houses of prayer,
Romano-Norman oracles, colonisers of the soul.

And once in the night, I could have sworn it
on oath, I caught the shadow of the blind harpist
groping his way through a harpsichord
of the great halls, the memory of his first love
a love bite bruising him.
In a moment of grace, in the light between land
and lake, O'Carolan cocks his head and cries:
this is the hand of Bridget Cruise.

IV

Through webs of sinning
through rain drizzling
through every genuflection and kneeling
through song of blackbirds and bluebells

as elusive as heaven's listenings
as instrumental and compelling

evidence of the mind's dis-ease:

the blackbird's game to alarm me
the texture of earth informing me

13

the palette of the lough to lighten me
flints of penance finetuning

breezes in my throat,
stars to my eyes in the night
lopping of the waves to my ears
winds from the South to my back

and dissonance of old ghosts
exposed on the shimmering island
singing the solemn of the Cross;

voices across the lough,
an anchored boat.

I renounce the World, the Flesh and the Devil.

V

A sudden gust caught me on the hop
letting me in on
                    countless recitations,
mantras reeled off by heart and the mechanical
freeing up of all my psychic places
where I dare to hallucinate by the lakeside,
                              see an arm rising
to break the surface with, I swear it, a bottle
of delirious Old Bushmills.

I could have endured
anything but the hordes of sleep pounding
on my brain, the ache for a begger's meal,
                    chilled shiverings of rain;

14

anything but their laced up shoes
and black soutanes and the stand-up comic
routines on the altar; the synchronised laughs
may God forgive them and acquired small talk
                                    about Aquinas and the like
who engineered such complexities
as to whether frogs were flesh or fish
and might be eaten on a Friday.

Aside, I compose another ghost,
poet in an overcoat,
                          pockets wedged
with a naggin of the hard stuff and thick slices
of bread; ham sandwiches for soakage,
scraps you wouldn't put in a mousetrap
and set that against the rigours of such a night,
                                    and the hungers for an open kiss
that tongues its humours into the cold.

VI

A dying wasp crawls up my coat,
a close-run thing, chameleon,
making for my throat.
Distracted from its laborious progress
on the ground, I found out, mortified,
it had me in mind :

through radiance of violence,
through craft of killing,
through pentametre of slander
and cool conniving,

through art of porn
and soft distortion;

jig-actors of the image
acting the goat with light,
three card tricksters training slivers
at chinks in the cloud.

The sun sours. We turn round
and around spinning in on ourselves
to lose the run of its track
hardly knowing whether we face it
or have it to our backs.

VII

Dawn shivers over the lough and over my fallen sleep.
An easy chair I chanced on thanks be to God
(the scrapings of the barrel of a prayer)
was upon my word of honour no temptation
but a just reward.

With the air of a sleeper, I walk to the water's edge,
bracing myself in its holy communion.
I begin again, dip my hand
in the offered waters of the lough
and bless myself
with the sign of the Cross
and the suddenly arrived question mark
of a single ray of sun.

The remainder I let go of: smudged rumours
left behind in bare footprints.

I gather up my things, ease myself back
into shoe leather on thick socks,
crisscrossing the laces in a pattern
topped by a double knot.
Without a second thought, I make for the boat,
the feet heavy, weighted down.

I renounce the World, The Flesh and the Devil turned Clown.

The weather will be cold all over Ireland
with patches of drizzle, and frost,
and sunny spells
and snow on high ground.

Prelude

In the garden of the Poor Clare convent
(a place of reticence, of undisturbed communion)
within a stone's throw of the old jail,
the Sacred Heart statue,
painted white,
addresses eternity in defense of now.

laudamus te

There is always that first movement
of perceived light racing across the weir
or trapped inside a bird's wing
prompting wanton song from decrepit January trees.
This is no time for dawdling beside water
in the wake of water hens and herons, detailing
frostways black as midwinter's night

where cars with dimmed headlights
wreak havoc among the rats.
Between the water and the mill
a hard oasis of penance;
old roots, an old jail, remnants of the old faith
fathom a metaphysical trick of the light —
statements of the Angelus or a question raised
in the hours before closing time:
Christmas, Candlemas, Lent.

adoramus te

Simultaneous Equations

The antique clock has cast its shadow
on the saffron smiles
of latterday customers, face
permanently fixed at twenty five minutes
to the midnight hour.

Among the bona fides, ready reflections
of a not-too-profound nature
bounce from snuff box to old whisky bottle,
words chancing a link-up:
collision, conjunction, cut.

In the ups and downs of fabulous banter
I notice silence in a Breughel print,
a smoke-washed, stunned cacophony
of once-upon-a-time.

Once I walked the walls of Acre,
remembering crusader knights
and the song of their pretence —
introibo, credo, sanctus.

Back at the bar, a code
of last orders, last calls securing
the necessary one-for-the-road

along which, rows
of Persian rugs distract
to image the radiance of your breaking

and I switch to another station,
informing chaos with direction; prepare
for presence.

Premonition

This is November's membrane —
a winter christening of stem,
greyveined stacks, pines dripping with ice

and driven by the east wind, an echo
of summer slipped its berth to the rosewood
of the parc anglais in Villequier,
quiet beside the river
where Hugo raged inarticulate,
prayers burnt to ashes of utterance, premonition
spent on a tidal surge, a capsized boat, a rage:

a de profundis roar.

Here, starlings swarm, skirting obsidian lakes
and skies of blue malachite,
impressionist fashion,
almost a stradivarius —
fluid in flight —
weeping catherine wheels
across the rationed fields of Advent.

On the Via Dolorosa

In an antique shop on the Via Dolorosa —
the sun knifing alleyways with surgical precision,

bronzes green with age
and artefacts dating from a time
before common era
(or BC if you like),
sophisticated fakes,
guaranteed authentic,
provenanced.

How many shekels,
how much does it cost?

The door behind you, lady, is locked.
Turkish coffee? Our tradition is one of ...
hospitality.

I watched the smile fade out fresco and jar,
Herodian oil lamps with handle and spout,
terracotta figurines and shards.

I could, if I so wished — it is in my power,
woman, you are in my sway —
abduct and rape, mutilate
and leave you to desert lizards,
suchlike. Woman from the West,
you do not know our way.

I watched the green bronzes,
sophisticated fakes —
How many shekels, how much does it cost?

21

(He hadn't heard my question, at first.)

Outside on the Via Dolorosa,
the sun had ripped deep shadows —
and passed.

Songlines

There's no doubt that the place was the same place;
it was the time was different
and something of congruence had occurred

and something had given :
ripped stitches, may be, that needed darning
even if my skill with a needle was always dodgy

to say nothing of the book I read
at the same time keeping one hand free to turn
the page, the other one all over the place in wool,

straining to unravel character and dialogue and plot
though nothing could have wised me up
for the sight of a dead tree in a summer field,

branches bleached like old bones lying around
on the look-out for answers;
left me with a question mark and a stone

inscribed in Irish which, loosely translated, means
that things are as they are, though the reason
why is still to play for

as the remembered dockers knew well
sitting on an idle wall, watching the sun go down
when they could see it for the rain,

dreaming of fine days and a good catch
and the luck fallen between them and calling
the drowned by name

a stone's throw away from where
I deliberately listen to the birds singing
as they've always done over Mallard's Lake,

reminding me of a day when I listened for nothing else.
It was summer, as it is now. And I was
walking away from something I couldn't

put my finger on, watching the driven lake
darkened by an almost gale force wind,
at a loss then and with no notion

that water, like calm, always finds its own level
but wary of the old wisdom hanging in the air,
words and then silence filling

with all the intimacies of a bog in winter
and the way it was downwind when the springer
winged across Crimlin Bog

and how easy it was to lose track of
the liver and white of his coat
against the dark cuttings and camouflage

but knowing how a clear whistle would turn him
from the scent like a sudden turn in the road
or a turn of phrase where language and contour merged

in the footprints of the tongue.
In the changing light of the same bog,
I try to colour in

the where
in which
I was.

After Beckett

Waiting for the news, waiting
for the unexpected —
that's how the year went
and the *fin de siècle*
with rumours of this or that apocalypse,
predictions of disasters or worse.
It's always the future that counts,
now is far too commonplace, too habitual
to allow for excitement or fear
or glimpses of an after-life,
if there is life after all . . .

This day, prematurely old,
bears all the signs of déjà-vu,
a stale preoccupation with chores —
time to feed the dog, roast decaying flesh,
a pinch of salt, a hint of garlic
and a spud . . .
and all shall be well.
You tell me to have patience and wait.
Don't you see there's nothing to wait for,
except death? Is that the promise
you refuse to articulate —-
thoughts that die before they're coffined
in words bound by the barbarous mystery of mind.

You remember that old man who waited
to be old before reading
all the volumes in his bookcase,
by which time he was, of course, blind?
Instead he listens for passing cars and footsteps

and is consumed by sound.
Now emptiness brings terror to his door —
silence rising and falling and still; and still
he knows the silence that precedes
and that which comes after.

In the end he grew even older and deaf to boot
and listens now in his head
and only occasionally cries out
when he hears his breathing
and mistakes it for the wind
in his half demented way
sitting by the window, his head inclined
to sunrise or sunset coming into being, then dying.

And all the while he waits, going over and over
the distant images of rancid time.
He sees clearly now the light in the light
of darkness; that was what he discovered.
The problem was to follow through in his shufflings
the crystal clear directions in his head,
which is to say . . .

In the last analysis,
it's all the same whether
I monitor his progress or not.
What's it to him
if I should write the captions
for his life?
He would, still, listen
to the sound of his own breathing,
and wait.

Sean-Nós

Is cuma. Your first words. You meant it by way
of modesty when we met on the dreamers' road, full
of potholes and bogholes and a question in passing
above the Lake of the High Waves
and that unexpected sight of old roses
trailing by the gable end of a vexed ruin.

Down by the *cladach*, the wind was picking up
like a word from the old language tracking its way in
from a muddied ocean, the tang of *sean-nós* in your throat
crying out for sound as if meaning had lost its way
between the lethal arms of sundew and shadowed bracken
where the almond scent of meadowsweet, wild water mint
and the thought of summer breaking almost stopped my breath.
In your eyes, too, the mackerel are running. *Aríst*.

• *Sean-Nós* = traditional singing   • *Is cuma* = it doesn't matter
• *cladach* = beach   • *aríst* = again

Grotto by the Lough

Out of the lifting grey of a late spring, they come
steadily, stillness already
in the way they negotiate the lowest step

to take their cue from the immutability
of the plaster cast figure,
mould of many forms, image holder by the lough

where isobars radiate out of memory
bearing vestigial prayer
and reticent nightlights slip, dipping, into the dark.

Like splashes of beeswax on silk:
plastic Grecian urns, off-white,
a basket of fake daisies, saxifrage and fern;

slabs pockmarked and fleeced with moss,
the limestone furrowed with all the flesh eaten off
the soft parts from raindrops dripping

implacable as a loveless marriage
(there were men too in these parts
who never married for want of work for a woman).

At a glance, the haphazard artistry of the casual
tips over into the sad staring into the far distance
of sunken eye sockets petrified by stills

of old drownings in summer sepia, gouged out
by weathering beside leftovers of the Romanesque:
a one-time window filched from some discarded churchyard

occasions the pedestrian batik work of the May altar,
the relief of hammer and chisel etchings,
candle drippings, strings of broken rosaries;

bluebells, cowslips and meadowsweet
crammed into jars are daisy chain illuminations;
the cinematic sequence of a May day.

Make no mistake about it — that single blackbird,
acrobat of the high notes, is singing his head off
for a gutsy lady in blue, out over the lough, beyond

the beyond and down the road,
after me, where I walked;
a tangerine sky, dust on the ground.

Summertime

The garden is overgrown
and summerwild almost to distraction,
almost to my front door:
its hardgloss coat of hollygreen

that opened to my quickened latchkey
all winter long gives in suddenly
to the fragility of night scented stock
in earthenware pots below the windows

and last year's tips
offloaded at random by lorries
looking for a dumping ground
are sprouting sweet rockets

by the breathful.

Old Scores

Stay tuned. Remember the last time the gate swung to,
enough in itself to contend with
besides that sinking in the pit of the stomach
that comes from a parting of the ways;

on putting the best foot forward, going over
old ground, slowly, the face dead set against
the heart's unease, hellbent on resisting the signals
that might have staved off that one false move.

On the swings and roundabouts of conjecture, I worry
Nephin's purple pulling on the threads
of old connections, the hammered common sense
of the stay put whistling in the wind.

So the lost box accordion still says it all, reeking
of old misery all the way back to the crossroads
where grandeur fought a last ditch stand
and lost its pitch to new gods. And novelties.

About Winters

If you were to ask about winters, I
would talk of breath hanging, brazen
as memories coming and going
through the air;

of summer rosebuds frosted
by November crystals,
and blackberries poised
to perish on the stalk;

of trees crippled
in the sculpted choreography
of light,

or an old springer
getting his second wind
in the scent of grouse and snipe;

shouts of children across lake water —
echoes in the bog, where stillness
and mist invert

my question.

But you fail to recognise
the praxis of decay, and I fall
short of brittle image,

fall into silence —
fall away.

Portrait

You have the air of someone
standing by a window —

as if the fix of a passing glance
had rooted you forever
in the foothills of listening,
valved you to strands
of gorgeous sunlight, dazzled
by fabulous currents.

And the shadows
you might have danced with,
the seawrack of the alternative,
slip below the tide line,
ride the waves, the breakwater shore.

Now, only the cold fingers of the verbal
can come crashing
on the allegation in your heart;
only, in absence, name you,
your passion for the back roads,
your foothold.

Surrendering to broken glass and shard
I tender sweet aloes, leave you
roses at the back door.

On the Reek

Staring me in the face : Clew Bay,
conscious of how it throws into relief
the mountain, holy by association, mysterious
as fresh footprints on bedraggled pathways;

the sheer grudgery of its hunched back
tightlipped in the face of the child's play at the base,
skipping to a rhythm that's all uphill, going straight
and in the right direction

until that first circle of second thoughts
turned me around to the weight of the world
on my back. Through fingers of light, I see my way
vaguely, look down on the gallery of islands

confusing them in the night for stars in the sky.

Ghost Story

There's a lightness in the air,
suggesting sun.
Winter lifts itself
from the shoulders of an April road.
A woman walks, head down, talking on her mind.
I notice growth again, dandelions
tumbling wildcats in the tired grass,
an easter stream racing to a clogged drain.

This was the road my father walked
with a ghost, a sworn story —
cross my heart —
of caution warmed by a winter's fire.
At the graveyard gates, where the road
narrows, she vanished from his sight —
a haunted soul, a sudden death, an unrepented sin.

It was not uncommon knowledge
that she walked, wanting charity,
the favour of a last requiem.
Purgatory was a hard place, they said,
much like Lough Derg, only worse.
I take the customary three steps
in the wake of a ghost, suggesting mercy:
cans of buttermilk, an old shawl, unconfided sin.

This road had its own history once
before television came, before
the sound of the soundbyte blocked out
all the inclinations of nuance;
possessed our telling with a mongrel song.

Before this happened,
we knew the narratives of night, how
to tell shadow from shadow, the
afterlife of one
who carried the milk to town, one
whose journey wasn't finished with a switch
on a stoneless tomb.

I notice runnels of growth —
ivory lace on the hawthorn,
fields coming out to an old consonance:
ceapach, fiodán, gort *
with which I envisage familiar ground
and sanctify the skies again —
not counting distance.

* fields

Time of Arrival

Somewhere —
the word in its precise definition
is waiting for release
like a row brewing
over some imagined right-of-way.
I test it for resistance and feel its pull.

Something came over me;
a quirk of direction and I lose sight
of a thing I thought I caught a glimpse of.
Was it a trick of the light
or some small confusion of the mind
danced over in another world?

I see nothing for it but the long haul,
the trawl for silver lists, namings
wedged between roof and tongue —
(the mayfly, wings delicate as breath,
lies nose down on the window sill)
but neither hard graft
nor the mind's toss for heads or tails
can draw it

from the dark, where the shaken up roots
of last year's African violets,
packed loosely in tabloids,
are constantly harping on earth
and a spring unwrapping,
and waiting

as, behind the turf stack, the Jack Russell
in a theatre of birth,

the pups already dead the owner reckons
and twice her size, his tight-lipped eyes
remarking country lore and cuteness
in matters of money, rebuke
the heart's requirements for a vet :
leave her alone, she'll bring them yet.

Going by all the signs, I argue
for the light, for clarity,
and wait with both hands watching
to hold it the first time it shows.
All loose intuition, I sense
something swim, resolutely, into my mind;

a powerful, loping stroke.

Genesis

In the beginning
there was chaos
in the clay of God's word;
in the shaping;

in the hammered out
legislation.

There was confusion of growth,
of knowledge tumbling
like fruit from an apple tree
when the season had come in.
Then I shouted "this is me, is where I'm at"
but blankness stared me back,
unminding.

Veiled at the face of my silence,
I ghost the windfall, the bruised flesh,
the core :

No words for the womb-men,
no score.

Second Thoughts

Qui tollis peccata mundi . . .

Surely it must have dawned
on him, then —
the realisation
that he was playing
a fool's part,
and the mighty heave
he undertook
in the interest of redemption
was just another detail
on the landscape of humanity,
resulting in a bland acceptance
for the sake of form . . .

miserere nobis.

Did he really think
to raise a pedestrian world
to sacramental status —
then —
when he tasted thirst?

Coming Down from Jerusalem

I imagined how it was
in your day, my feet
gathering dust by the waters
you walked on; looking for ways
out of the old city
you wept over.

I can see how the desert
must have beckoned, the need
to escape the clamouring crowds
looking for a god
at any cost.

There was a cross —
before they lashed you
to their image, a male
and righteous God,
defined your creativity
in a bundle of rods.

Somehow your space suffers them
to crush —

somewhere there is pure movement,
unmoved —

and sometimes, a carolling
of linguistic music unmarked
by language —
fumbles through.

Oil on Canvas

With cadence
of a requiem in your soul,
you hold the chemistry
of old energies
played out under dark
gothic arches; spill
cathedral echoes
onto canvas.

In the glosses
of manuscripts,
you meet
the master builders,
resonance of old bells
and pilgrims mourning : transpose
their music
to a new medium.

Finding vision
in the charcoal,
you leave crimson marks

in bright sunlight.

Still Life

You hold your cross
like some nonchalant tennis player,
bearing those red gashes
like badges of artistic triumph;
lacquered wounds made sensuous
on the edge of a palette knife
in colours of burnt sienna and crimson
and ochre
under a glaze of wafered dust,
looking almost pretty
in ornate frames;
each cartoon
a blow by blow account
of your trip
from Gethsemane to Calvary,
artist or artists unknown.

Dispassionate among the bones,
we settle in the shadows
of an Easter Saturday,
back to back,
pencilled between a christ
impaled on the pain of centuries
and the scorched epiphany
of lightened stone.

Lightfalls

Breathtaking in repentance, the light —
lovely after rainfall —
is a staggered act of consummation;
stills in the quenching of a thousand candles.

You strike me — traipsing after signs —
as too exclusive for words,
preferring to leave footprints in silence
or daub the sky with your signature.
I stare at the stars, allow for distance,
detect nothing. You whisper
and are far off.

I turn to black crows knifing twigs,
gauging breath and balance
in creation's horoscope, nudging

winter's reticence from the hard clay,
while spring shimmers the air
like beaded raindrops
in unexpected sunlight.

Winterscape

In the sun, trees
like scarecrows, old sticks
clinging to hard soil, witness

a moment of redemption, a tangle
of tinselled gold falling
on the distant bones

of a jagged landscape, faces
angled from the East, a scene
from Caravaggio, souls struggling
in half light

and conscious always of cold, coming
through walls and into rooms,
carried in on coats, and in the chill
of breathing

I feel another kind
of cold, watching a child
fully grown and reaching
to know the mystery of knowing, eyes
pools of everlasting innocence.

Knowing, I bury my face
in the fragrance of warm bread,
seek the comfort of warmed sheets,
curse the absence of sleep.

Island

Raked by shifting cloud,
the planets in alignment
held off facing down

as tides tumbled across my reading,
chapters of menace smashing
against black rock —

praise thrown back
in relentless ricochet; image
of a raw-boned god
along cliff faces springing pink lichen,
in crimson butterflies on a country road,
the yellow tormentil of bog —

a palette splintered
by the lowing of seals in hiding.

Wracked to a rhythm my shoulders
learnt to know, I wrestled
with the worst of crosswind; bartered
text for song.

The island huddled
where I stood
facing elemental rages, head-on.

Silhouette

Locked in the record of my coming,
the world was awash with newness, twigs
thickening to a green mould, your journey
to abandonment underway.

You moved in moments of lucidness
eccentric to my milieu, subverting stillness
in stony ruins; a way without, bringing

chrism of chisel to unsculpted stone.

I fear
no call to root out words
from the hardened arteries
of a breathless mind;

I fear
seething currents clawing
at a coal black sea; suffocation
on the back of burdened song.

I fear
your shadow on the ground.

Exultet

I tossed back the memories
when they came, blocked out
the image-maker's game. Dead as old fur
they stopped breathing in me.
Staccato-wise, the rains came
tracking an Easter song uphill
to where the prism tumbled
light to colour.
Breathe now. Countenance down
the breathlessness of life
that tumours on the Cross.

Receive his soul.
Present him to God Most High.

I am light shining through the stained glass
windows of the past,
a candle guiding form to energy
to die in mouse grey blobs of fat.

Angels of God, come to his aid —
Come to receive him, Angels of the Lord.

Your God seems a little odd
by all the standards of the day,
given to long silences
and not really into customer relations
or the hard sell.
Packaging is the bottom line —
everyone knows that now
and the Jansenist approach won't wash

anymore. The people
know best, after all
they buy the product
amd he ought to understand the market
and its structures.

Hezekiah did not sleep dreamless.
Outside the walls, Sennacherab preyed
on Judah's soul —
(Lackish laid waste in purple moonlight)
chiselled water stilled in the pool of Siloam,
water spun of ointment and balm.
Who is that figure, heavy shrouded, waiting
by the pool?
When did he come?

Dust in the pencilled path
of a nucleus, a soured infusion falling out —
earth losing sight like an old Zachary
wary of life. Who
would be dead?

He is risen, as
he said.

Song of Caedmon

In the beginning, there were
lashings of words spilling over, racing
to discover all the vacant spaces
that only words can chart.

But little by little
pauses came
and punctuation,
and the words served
as workmen's tools —
nothing more.

And later still, there
was the language of profound thought
to test the waters.

After which,
there was only silence.

And all the while, Caedmon
waited.

On the Bridge

Only forty three when he folded his coat,
climbed across railings
and jumped from the bridge
at two in the morning
when the drink was corked, the nightclub
closed, and silence jostled out
the loud narcotic throbbing
of everyone else's joy.

Then he left. Nailed
to the cross of indifference, he couldn't
cross that bridge.

What did he think
as he fell from one reality
to the next? To cinnamon waters
down and out
of step with numbed windows and rooms
where, muffled and warm, all good people
were turning over for their second sleep,
turning their faces to the wall,
safe in the dark?

Out on the bridge, see
the tide stagger with a shadow
on its back.

Pietà

A curving of form
cased in glass
against weathering
and vandal's hammer.

Stone grief compelling
quiet —

a timeless stunning,
extraordinary moan,
redemptive timing.

Wanton tourists pin its spray
to their labels, checking out
pierrot's trail.

This is Rome, St. Peter's
where Michelangelo's gaze
fell —

where figures of Bernini, frozen
in mobility, are silent
by an unseen hand.

Lady, you hold in faith
this vast expanse of pain, wreckage
from a cosmic cross —

chisel in a glass case.

Desert Perspective

Speaking of holy writ, there is no vision
to separate the teller from the tale.

There were campfires, after we had gathered dung
and withdrawn. Then they sat to warn listeners
with stories from the mind of God. Language
was theirs. It was fitting they should speak.

There was no revelation for us. Tied
to compliance, we had no time to conjure
a sympathetic god.

Though his coming gave us pause —
the desert's latent power crossed
nomadic knowledge to his gospel.

When he died, it was the tentmaker
who picked up the image; fleshed it
to his own design.

It was not a question for the Council,
they enlightened us with souls, the Fathers
of Nicaea : fashioned by authority —
majority of one.

       *   *   *

My people, what have I done to you?
How have I offended you?

Answer me!

Listen, the time came
when all their tribal customs
disappeared like dung in the desert.
But I was alive, and breathing

a question —
though prejudice pinned me
like a broken butterfly,
labelled me virgin, mother, whore;

assertion —
though your silence
colluded in my paralysis, damned
me to his board;

sentence —
only to myself
since your bread has a price
and must still be taken at their word.

Cameo

I saw the comet —
caught between Orion
and the one they call the Plough,
its long trail blazing into dreamtime.

Dawn saw it off —
the haze hallowed and held,
the sun with its pale agenda
transfigured frost to flame.

Stunned, I take strands
of ragged thread over to your window,
waiting on your word;
pick potsherds from the ruins
of burn-out, attempting
light in dark earthenware;

watch waves splashing
across lake stones,
a fine embroidery,
a threading of repeated things,
tossing and turning

and in the dusk of peppered
stars, clouds teeming
with burnt wax, I listen
to your absence

breaking the sky apart.

Idiocy

A bit touched they called him
and consequently unable
to utter independence
but leaning heavily on the demon
that possessed him,

he held back
aware only of awe
and of others trampling
on mystery.

In the Ordinary Way

Why did you force my hand,
forge in pain a meetingplace,
place of confrontation —

wrest rhyme from the dark earth
of poetry, hacking from the rock
of language a single thought
worth expression —

raise your standard and depart?

Once when rain bled the branches
to impressionist haze outside my window,
I could marvel then at your derangement,
touch the hieroglyphics of your hand.

Searching for oddments, I find images
of hope colliding with time:
the light leftovers of a winter's evening.
But needing the comfort of the commonplace,
I turn to convention,
undertake the ordinary,
carry on.

In the clearing of my mind,
a gathering of music speaks its gradual.

Ashes

Conscious of the interminable, I
become impatient with your obstinate
absence, tire of endless questions
and the rhetoric of mystery.

Famished, I visualise
discordant notes, scores
of thunderous drumming fused
with sparkling strips of lightning, and

fallen quiet, endorse your furious tension
working itself out in a flash
of human fire, blazing
a divine extravagance to smash
the tedium of grey.

Here also you are unpredictable,
refuse to be drawn
even by indignation
or honest outrage.

You transform nothing.
We hunch by warmed ashes
drawing diagrams
of pain.

Unscripted

I sensed you, variously
still —

not in written script or
old books of strict
commandment;

not in chronicles of love
where you were
absent;

not in my own time
or precarious places
of my way

but in the even descant
of the ordinary: the slow chorale
of gathered silence where I
stumbled into stillness,

stood in the crowd
and watched, wary
of your loveliness, prized you
from afar
in fine editions of evening
distance. On reflection,
somewhere

you drew a bow
across my deafness. I heard
no music

when you opened up gethsemane
and came to me

in poetry.

Shabat

All I remember now
of a far shabat
is that crude division
of the Wall,
the greater part reserved
for fathers, sons and brothers,
husbands and lovers,
leaving the rest —
for the rest.

There I took my place
and turning to the Wall, prayed
an unremembered prayer:
a scrap of paper
surreptitiously fingered
and squeezed into rock —
finding breath in a crevice.

Dóchas

Ar nós fréamhacha
faoi chlúdach i bpáipéar nuachtáin
i gcónaí ag súil le breith
agus an tEarrach,

tháinig mearbhall orm
faoi ghleacaíocht an tsolais
agus an racht cainte
atá in ndán dom.

Outlook

In the manner of roots
wrapped in newspapers
awaiting birth
and the Springtime

I grow besotted
by the movement of light
and the outburst
that's in for me.

Grafadh

Mar ghluais
ar imeall na lámhscribhínne,
mar adhlacadh
thar chiorcal na cloiche,
mar chosc
ar bhealach na gréine,
mar lasair,
as láthair,

faighim coiscéim
in ábhar lofa an phortaigh,
lá geimhridh
agus an ghaoth
ag baint fuarallais
as mo chuimhne —
glan díreach
ós mo chomhair amach.

Imprint

Like a gloss in the margin
of a manuscript,
like a burial
beyond the stone of the circle,
Like the blocked passage
of the solstice,
Like illumination,
and absence, and un-ease,

I find footprints
in the rotting composition
of Crimlin Bog
on a winter's day
as the wind throws old memories
back into my face.

Ag Tóraíocht an tSolais

Gualainn a chuir mé chun dorais,
an ceo céanna a bhí ar oscailt
dóibh siúd atá scaipithe sa chré;
go bhfeice mé an seansolas.

Ach ní faoiseamh a bhí i ndán dom ach ceist;
cogar a bhíos ag stealladh uaireanta
agus uaireanta ag fáil bháis
ar aon leis an ngealach.

Ar nós oíche Nollag fadó a thagann an sólás
(beannaithe ar an taoide)
gan focal a chur orm
ach séimhe a bhfuil teacht agam air
i rith na hoíche:
ganntanas sa chaint,
an briathar romham,
mé ag iarraidh labhairt.

Footnote

I fill my mouth with the vowels
of those whose tongues are clay
in the hope of breaking through
back into the old light,
an idiom hard to come by.

It's as well for me to listen to the moon
throwing shapes at hidden phrases
in the light of which, I stammer to get started
and put my tongue to a syntax
that my people lived and died by.

Ráiteas

Ar an oileán,
ar maidin,
bhreathnaigh mé sall,
ag iarraidh freagra ón ngála.
Ní fhaca mé
ach cruth na ndall ar an aigéan
's an ghaoth ina gealt.
"Force Nine, déarfainn"
arsa fear a' bháid
agus ba chuma leis sin,
a thóin sáite i dtine na tábhairne,
gloine fuisce á cháitheamh siar aige:
"tá an chosúlacht ann
go mbeidh muid ag dul amach.
Ach, beidh an lámh in uachtar againne —
feicfidh tú —
is ná bí buartha faoi".

Ar an gcéibh,
tráth nóna,
'éis fuaim na mara
bheith báite ag an mbodhrán,
bhris an fuacht ar an slua
's iad ag dul amach,
sa chaoi gur shéan siad an talamh
agus duine i ndiaidh a chéile,
thug siad cluas
do ráiteas doicheallach na dtonnta.

Smalltalk

One look at the weather and I would have cried off
and clung to the island - no matter what.
And if the wind went mad in the bay and beyond
and the breakers rammed the cliffs,
there was more than enough shelter
by the turf fire in the pub, as the boatman remarked
with a casual nod at the quivering windows
and the door about to burst open at any moment;
"force nine, I'd say" he began, as if
it were all the same to him
what with his arse stuck in the fire
and a half one downed and ready for a refill:
"but don't worry, we'll master her",

and we knew, all of a sudden, that no bodrán
could drown out the sound of the waves
and no easy talk could get in the way of the gangplank
swinging madly between bollard and boat —
as we waited to go out.

Ceol Johnny Phadraig Pheter

Dhearc mé siar,
fuascailt a fháil
ó bhagairt na farraige
agus achainí na ndaoine
i ngéibheann sa mbád.
Ar tí 'bheith tinn
('s is olc an tinneas é)
tháinig ceol chugam ar an ngaoth
ós cionn cleataireál na mbád
agus achrann na taoide
agus an dream ag déanamh imní faoi.

Lá samhraidh doininne,
idir Inis Bó Finne
agus an Cloigeann,
bhain muid aicearra amach
ar dhroim cheol choisricthe an bhoscadóra.

Crossing

I looked back, thinking to find
something to hold on to
from the disappearing back
of the island, already
a world away from the grasping hands
of an outstretched sea
and the sickness that threatened
to overwhelm me,
when I heard it —
music becoming entangled with the wind
and coming between me and the seaweed water.

On such a day in Summer,
on a crossing between Inisbofin and Cleggan,
a shortcut opened up
through the closed eyes of a boxplayer.